MY LIFE IN HEAVEN

For michele —
with best wishes
for you — and your poems!

Mary Ann

May 20, 2013

MY LIFE IN HEAVEN

MARY ANN SAMYN

Oberlin College Press
Oberlin, Ohio

The FIELD Poetry Series, vol. 29
Oberlin College Press, 50 N. Professor Street, Oberlin, OH 44074
www.oberlin.edu/ocpress

Cover and book design: Steve Farkas
Cover photograph: Mary Ann Samyn

Library of Congress Cataloging-in-Publication Data

Samyn, Mary Ann, 1970-
[Poems. Selections]
My life in heaven / Mary Ann Samyn.
    pages cm. — (The FIELD Poetry Series ; vol. 29)
Poems.
ISBN 978-0-932440-45-7 (paperback : alk. paper) —
ISBN 0-932440-45-2 (paperback : alk. paper)
I. Title.
PS3569.A46695M95 2013
811'.54—dc23
                                                2012043287

Contents

June for Good

Little Muchness

The Moon Through a Skylight

Let's Be Serious Now

Men's bodies are interesting.

One thought or another on a long day.

I was being watched, mildly, from afar.

The story lay in wait; I'd not been there.

The falconer said: birds fly from hunger.

Careful; all's forgiven.

For no reason, *long ago* reappears, handwritten.

The guitar riff I've always wanted to be starts up.

Jesus—

Let the metaphors commence.

Just Say When

To hell with it shook the day.

A mouse came loose; the cat had dibs;

palest June continued, just to be sure.

A little pool of *shush*—no matter

what they tell you—is not a strategy.

And to think, already,

I hadn't been so easy to live with.

At Glen Lake vs. *The Birth of Anger*

Briefly put, I was spring-fed,
like many a lake.

For his part, Jesus slept a lot,
while others worried.

Returning home isn't easy;
no one said it would be.

Talk about comfort zones,
sticky sadness—

The children drew chalk crucifixes,
two versions; please vote.

All around the lake, tiki lights mean
someone's making a party.

Good for him is what I thought;
I'll pray to that.

Speaking of Ferocity at Sunset

Some clapped, and what I felt came and went,
an old song, so I sounded like myself,
again, years ago, singing in the basement,
wanting out. To bide one's time means
keep hoping. I gleaned a lot by pouting, more
by not. Considered escape mechanisms:
the river's is the lake; the lake's, *never-you-mind.*
A wind soothes itself, which is not nothing.
Try it, you might like it; I missed him too, but
the point was beauty, briefly put,
the sun the model of *leaving, not left.*

The Key Is How

Dappled light is neutral.
Painted dappled light, useless, mostly.
What had been successfully avoided might have helped,
actually, given the chance.
I walked from one lake to another, not choosing.
"We're on a ship now," the all-alone sisters told each other,
covering themselves: "Good night, good night."
Mid-afternoon: what's not to love?
The dunegrass sways, and is sharp.

The Moon Through a Skylight

A wing on a shelf, somewhat functional,
like a lady's fan, or another era.
And on the underside of each feather, a spine:
yellow like a secret.
All of it, a leftover altar, not mine.
Mine is all stones, including the one shaped like a heart.
"You're certain, aren't you?" someone asked,
though I felt told.
And later when he dropped the word *regards*,
I picked up even that, and added to my little stash.

Shark Shark Shark, or Whatever It Is That You Want Next

I had been slow to anger. I had been

slow, to anger.

Then, the beach curved as promised on the postcard.

Nothing to do with anybody.

And the children who had none

invented danger.

Likewise, for once I allowed my mind to wander.

Either way, ask me again in three months.

Octoberish

Run and tell all of the angels,
this could take all night.

—Foo Fighters

In Answer to Your Burning Question

It was a minor panic, thanks. It was a mirror
over the fireplace and I watched us.
It was the one a.m. train; I know because

I'm lonely. It was the usual awkwardness,
you claimed, though I'm not sure, really.
Rain in the air. And then, rain.

And snow back home; the map proves it.
Six a.m.: ok, if you want. We'll walk
in the dark. Or, stay here, also in the dark.

I'm Telling You the Story of Right Now

A hundred other things came first.
A thousand scraped knees, etc.

And I prayed real hard.

Fast forward: your wink lit me up.
And again: rainy October, no sky to speak of.

I wasn't imagining a better anything.

As for the footnote you requested, how's this:
just your name, repeated, like I said it.

You Got Your Wish; I Got Mine

A cheer goes up. Then, down, of course.
Other people deciding what more they want.

I'm no lonelier than I've been. Maybe less.
At church, suffering and ransom, another recap.

"Is that how we do it?" my mother asks,
meaning, as usual, God knows what.

Today's sun is buttery, is *never-you-mind*;
my attention span is shot. So, bravo, OK?

And just for the record, I made it look effortless.
Behind the scenes was another story.

The photo of this moment would break your heart.
Don't, not even for one minute, doubt that's true.

Octoberish

The scent of honeysuckle diagnosed me months ago, and
   predicted this.

Now, a different season entirely.

Maybe just one more was my thought about kissing you while
   you slept.

Urgency is noisy, sometimes.

Little by little, the next day's mood was inevitable as geese
   headed south.

Careful had been my other thought.

The story I caught myself telling myself was loud too, and total
   bullshit.

Thank God I realized.

Then parallel parked twice. Beautifully. On a hard day. For
   pride's sake.

It was a regular afternoon.

On the 5th, I wrote *why do you ask?*. On the 15th, *I won't soon
   forget it.*

And tonight, *a fine blue sky.*

Like an old envelope. Linen, maybe. Sealed with a waxy initial,
   and a wish.

Open it, of course.

Some things need to come from someone else's mouth to make
sense.

I learned that.

And learned, too, my limit—speed, everything to me once.

You Can Thank Me Later

—*Or now*, suggested November, seductive-like

and strangely warm; I couldn't get my bearings.

Judging by the prevailing mood, I'm guessing

this weather will continue for some time,

at least privately. Privately is best, anyway,

in my experience. *Take this off, take that—*

I was wanting some scientific reassurance.

In the dark woods there are no streets.

That's the page I opened to, 3rd edition

readiness for the future, *far and near.*

But the man is not lost. He can find his way.

Sweetheart, the man is not lost.

Happy Birthday, Everything!

The woods are full of birthdays.

Hip-hip-hooray for that.

And for me, pretty pleased

when I'm not doubting it.

I was a known quantity, kind of.

Like the pink in the trees

I wanted you to see—

Yes, my heart was broken; it was.

Now, let me try again:

the woods are full of animals.

The fact is, they're hungry.

Tell Me Something Good

What can occur, does, for once.

I'm happy.

What does gravity have to say about it?

No one needs to be a genius.

Page 39 says *Now try it this way.*

I watched you coming and going.

This is a record of that.

#5: You handled me.

#6: You handled me.

Mix, mix, mix: men like to make concrete.

The book says that too.

Now I know why.

You say I require a strict approach.

Let's see if you are right.

Want and Need

I'm considering delight, first and foremost, then and there.

Also, what happened to the sky when I went out to meet it.

Sometimes I arrive with a little childhood on me still.

The results are predictable. But what else *could* happen?

The man in the straitjacket wanted my attention and got it.

Just a magic show and many clapped to find themselves there.

Outside, the sweet gum suggested lucidity as a way of being.

God doesn't bother me, and your hand *right there* was perfection,

so I think I can do it. Likewise, *simultaneity* was in the air.

Meaning, you're thinking my name; this is no time to panic.

Cup and String

Flesh and Language

Then I saw firsthand and understood.
The hard day mingled with true power.

    —OK, I got it.

The feeling was *more particularly*.
The feeling was *discreetly* in a good way.

I was mostly *Mary Ann.*

Think on it.

What had been a tragedy was now a sigh.

I let my eye rest on the not-broken shell
brought back from the land of metaphor.

And then I knew:
allure doesn't come along every day.

Fascinated Is More Like It

In the *Primavera*, restraint is the point easily missed.

By way of contrast, I've been lovely on and off.

Better to be patient, I found myself telling myself.

I spent months in the meadow of that painting.

There, Venus is an adult. I know; it's tempting.

I'm happy to report I'm relinquishing some control.

So forget the allegory and tell me what you love.

For instance, I'm back here, in the grove of contentment.

Take It Back

—I said to the fear, just beginning.

Then dropped a dollar in the slot and lit a candle
at the feet of the bluest Madonna.

So I was fine, and when I wasn't, I didn't fake it.

It was fame that sat me beside my own photo to calm down.
And fame, too, means you think of me, more privately.

My instincts are good.

Now, the three a.m. train says *take heart*—

                              and the deer,
not moving in real life and not moving in dreams, agree.

Let Me Introduce You

You said *ka-pow!*—an explosion
with an explosion around it—
just as I touched the calluses on your hand.

Shadowbox this moment like I know you will.

Then turn around to see December, the last leaves
like a little heartache in the trees.

Indirection as a strength isn't, really, I know now.
But its opposite might not be either.

Regardless, the day was a bet and you won it.

And the river is blue for a change.

And the thing about advice is, the one who gives it
can take it, too.

More Perfect

"There, there," said the storybook mother. "That must have hurt."

But that was then; close it.

—Now, let's reflect:

> The leaf you saved—the littlest—was the one I thought was me.
> The first Christmas lights say *hey there*—, and on cue I wonder.
> Tonight's moon is the real deal. Did you see it too?

And the theory was clock time was one kind; love, another.
This is the action of telling: *we were taken by surprise*—

This is a gray area.

So guess what, darling?

Little known fact: you can have what you want.
This morning's robin, brilliant in the snowy hedges, told me so.

And I'm telling you in the tenderest way I know.

I Know You Know

What can be easily acknowledged already has been.

Check. Check. Check.

And yes, this thing is on and how we look is fact now.

I tried to notice the river's moods without getting involved;
I cooked the most delicious dinner;
I said "congratulations" and blew a kiss—

Now run away, if you can, and think it over.

This rain is lovely and I'll be fine, as I've been, meantime.

Cup and String

I'm pressing my ear to a wall of snow.
I'm a huntress in this dream, but it's just a dream.

In real life I've never been so patient.
Beauty, nature, violence, and love were on my mind.

There is no pre-existing story; I just like to watch you.
In comparison, fear is small. It is.

Those berries and that sunset are doing it in winter.
How's that for determination, satisfaction?

Now, are you calling? Good. Hello. Don't make us wait.
Pull the string taut—this isn't a toy—let's talk.

Please Do

What begins as a question ends as a declaration.

The five a.m. train agrees: that's how it goes.

Much like me, crawling across the bed.

Sometimes not-touching is almost touching.

Like when I wrote a note and tucked in the book.

Like when you wanted to kiss me in the hallway.

Soon enough Christmas comes, and maybe

a very pretty snowfall from me to you.

Don't doubt what you love; gratitude orders the day.

.

A Little January

The thoughts that came to her… were not really thoughts at all—
they were more like alterations in her body.

*

…Whether he touches her or not, whether he speaks to her or not.
He is pulling her to him, studiously attending to the job.

—Alice Munro

This Is the Forest; Do You Like It?

So we were speaking of God always, already:

my hand on yours, yours somewhere on me.

I thought I had been brave enough for a lifetime,

but I'm writing this out loud as I drive,

voice memo to the Ohio sunset I know you know.

Slowly slowly slowly is what I learned by rushing,

all my outcomes surprising *and* inevitable.

One of last year's last thoughts was *I'm fine.*

Here's a selfish hope you're just a little not.

New Year's *oh my*— arrives, and my *oh help*—.

And the pines, the pines offer their usual wonder.

True for Good

The sky had gotten whiter while we talked. A snow sky
out one window, a regular sky out the other.

Later someone would say to me: this is why people pick daisies
and pluck the petals one by one.

But just then I was busy making it worse. Talk about peril
further unsettling what desire had started.

So perfect, yesterday's snowflakes must have been cut from a book
and laid gently down. Was it you? I meant to ask.

But now I've made a deeper ache on a Thursday, Thursdays
having been so lovely all that fall.

The forecast says… something… but I can't quite remember;
I'm sorry, but I wasn't listening.

A Little January

It was all natural. The ideal world.

That cardinal just catching my eye;

snow on the roof making a new pattern.

When I remember, I believe.

I listened to your message again.

Hidden from view means only that.

Each month is instructive in its way;

this one is supposed to be chilly.

And this blue is called *high noon*.

One coat later, I stand back to see.

A Painted Sun

A harmless-enough-looking sun.

A sun of just three strokes.

And anyone can do it.

You think I'm kidding.

But not about this.

Also, sometimes I speak unkindly.

Snow blows in the open window.

A logical result.

Falling in love, similarly.

What can be accounted for has been.

Now you learned the lesson.

This is for real.

See: I'm squinting into it.

As a Consequence

Is that gonna work?, I asked the teeny-tiny snowflakes.

Not to introduce doubt into the situation, but come on—

I'd heard about this kind of love. Uncalculated. Windy.

And of course I too admire a clean beginning.

In the dream, I was the softest kitten ever left unattended.

Now confess what you will, and look at me.

There's effort and then there's effort, said the very cold day.

I've gone with fear before, but you deserve a braver me.

Understand? I'm just asking you to imagine.

Technological

I do the hour in three-minute intervals
like the hostesses on TV who sell the weather.

There wasn't really any new snow, after all.

And that whole last year was going through the motions.

You be in charge of it for a while I wanted to say.
Then did.

Facts are facts; power, power.

Some statements just become more and more true.

In the dream, the freight train went by already,
and the passenger train wasn't coming.

Real life sirens woke me early.

Innovation, sweetheart, is my bread and butter.

But this love, first thing in the morning
or lights out, I'm learning, is old-fashioned.

In the Process of Making It Better

Here's your proof: *Oh Oh Oh*: pink clouds in a row.

You didn't make me cry, but I did, a little, OK?

So are you comfortable, can I get you anything?

All January we've been edgy, together and apart.

When I read the beautiful story, I thought of you.

When I thought the dirty thought, you then too.

This is not about turns, you said. Remember?

I got my mind around that, fast, so kiss me soft.

Or hard, if you want. God, they say, is in the details.

Look this way, look that: a wind controls the coast.

It says: there's no reason to stop; why stop.

Wouldn't It Be Dreamy?

The current goes where it wants. You told me.

The flipside of anger is heartache. Everybody knows.

So let the record show, this sky is a compromise.

And let me rest my head, again, on your chest.

What waiting is for, I don't know. I was good.

The old timey advice is *say thanks, say goodnight.*

Also, *did you show him you liked him?* Oh yeah; I did.

Sometimes it's like I'm looking into the past:

a little grit from the sea stays in the shell.

Or into some sweet future today's blue jay suggests:

beauty and mischief, a space in the hedge:

who wouldn't want to fly into it? Let's make up.

Far as I Can See, Near as I Can Tell

Far as I Can See, Near as I Can Tell

Hush, you said, an imperative—*stop it*—or

like before: *there's no place I couldn't kiss you*—

So, yeah, the body knows and readies itself.

How's that for passionate thinking?

I bet a dollar you knew my mind and you did.

And now this missing is a hell of a thing to do.

That's been life, you said, both of us in winter sun.

The days are getting noticeably longer, you said.

And I answered with a report about the moon.

Some Kind of Lifetime

Love the regret too, said the beachy debris, a photo of *way back
when.*

When I did, a little inward *OK* happened, and I sighed into it.

Sighed, too, at that other opening caused by even your sleepy
hand on me.

Believing is always the beginning; every great tradition says so.

By way of example, the icicles formed and fell out of necessity.

And it's not too soon either to say I'm loving also your secret
heart.

So negotiate with yourself. As for me, I knew it when I wrote it.

By the Way, *Hello*

A day of waiting, and a room for it.

Ghosts on TV, and the urge to cry.

What should I do now, or next?

And why did I do what I did for so long?

A floral pattern catches my eye.

The ceiling curves like a sky, palest blue.

I'm loving you this very minute, OK?

Nothing is preventing anything.

What Do You Mean *What Do You Mean*—?

The evening recommended itself, first and foremost.

I tried it on and on. I told myself *none of this is bad.*

Then gathered what I could remember: smallness, mostly.

And stood back to see the little crushing heap.

What could I offer and to whom and for how long?

The new birds gave perfection a shot, sweetly.

I'm growing bold—*just you wait*—by listening.

Stupidity, Crabbiness, Moorings & Love

One possible Jesus was Jesus, stubbornly.

For argument's sake, the clouds moved very fast.

Good show! I wanted to say.

The clarity is inside you is what I said instead.

The professor and students nodded yes, and no.

Like when your mouth opened against mine.

Keats was awfully young when he wrote those letters.

I am frequently reminded.

What can I say? Seduction c. 1819 still sounds good.

The worst of it is mostly private.

Of what I asked myself.

Then snapped a photo in the hotel mirror.

It's Never Just a Minute with You

You'd think I'd be afraid.

The bear in the dream thought the same thing.

And I did begin this life married.

But who hasn't gathered twigs at dusk? *Please.*

Lack of faith is a problem with a solution.

A hard winter? Yes, sir.

A crooked smile? I've got one.

Nothing goes to waste. Not even shyness.

So here's a gift of pinecones you can count on.

Here's me, leaving the room.

And you watching, like you want, in *three, two, one—*

A Question and Its Answer

A girl and a castle meet; this is not yet a problem.

Then a beautiful lake intervenes.

This is our story, already in progress.

Isn't it obvious I'm most myself when you're in me?

There, I said it.

Maybe the forsythia, just out, deserves partial credit.

An epiphany if ever there was one.

Now, I could look at you a long time. Let me.

Bluebell Report

Do You Want Me to Parse It Out?

The night we slept beneath the painting, the river, a real one, for
　　once didn't flow north, but radiated from us.

Talking in the dark made it so.

Later I asked the buds on the sweet gum, *When did this begin?*
　　and they answered *more god.*

Now I'm saying it as simply as I can.

The painting is *Gray and Gold*; the decision was made before we
　　knew; I'm scared; intimacy, too, stretches in every direction.

A Covered Bridge

The breeze said *no, like this*—, and I gave it some time.

Last week's scenic detour is still on my mind.

When you read to me, you were already lovely.

These are the considerations of a day.

In the diorama: feather + cap gun + postcard of a couple kissing
   on a hammock.

In the real world, broken glass and magnolias make the same
   point.

I'm sensing fear.

But fear is not a problem; I'm not doing anything for fear.

I Had My Castle Before You Had Your Fortress

Write as though you're writing to someone
who understands everything.
　　　　　　　—Jean Valentine

Far from home, I needed the comfort only I could give, so I
　　dreamed you wrote me a letter.

Sweetheart, that's a compliment; I'm coming to you happy.

The fear is, the fear is, I know what that fear is.

And yeah, our separate back-thens were bad.

But this morning, two blue jays. And at the museum, totem
　　poles. My raven and your eagle.

Then a sky I knew by heart and wished your way.

The most embarrassing lovely thing keeps happening to me and
　　you're the first to know.

I'm crying the cleanest tears ever. Out of nowhere. Five minutes
　　and done.

I'm grateful beyond measure.

When I tore that fucking castle down, I did it with you in mind.

So that's why you, why now.

And in the honest-to-God parking lot, there was a sign—*each*
　　new day begins at midnight—and I wanted to tell you. I knew
　　you'd understand.

She Named It Beauty

So it got easier when I stopped believing everything I thought
and took a drive just because that might feel good.

Even the new loneliness was pretty nice and calmed me,
like the cherry blossoms when they fell.

I'd been unhappy here *and* there, I realized,
which set me down gently.

And ordering a bouquet for someone else, I knew what I'd prefer;
the actual flowers could come later.

There is no safety; your heart may break. Mine may.
I think all art is about this.

Perfection never did much interest me, but I have to ask:
are you seeing this sunset?

Bluebell Report

Beneath the false cypress and the quaking aspen I wonder what
will make it better.

One bush has a hole in its side, like Jesus; a bird does the work
of my hand.

Yesterday you said tomorrow. Today you're not so sure. "Only
God can make a tree."

One report is, *I'm crushed if you're doubting.* The other, *there were
no bluebells.*

It's Not a Poem, It's a Novel

The first goldfinch is a good omen: you can have it.

Falling in love, too, happened early.

When I noticed the full moon, the noticing itself felt good.

When I asked myself a gentle question, I got a gentle answer.

Yes: be patient; look at the river; take a hint.

Can we absolutely know? No.

I drove around alone all last summer narrating summer to you.

Closeness began to be accurate then.

Again with the Honeysuckle

Forever and Ever and Ever

A little warning bell goes off inside where what's good begins.
I go back a year. No—I can't. *Thank God—*

Tenderness says *there's just a little missing; don't fret.*
Like the leaf with the bite out of it; someone won't go hungry.

Now I'm moving rapidly through the memory.
Sometimes I screamed into the center or lay awake all night.

I got what I came for is a sentence about leaving.
For the longest time I mostly stayed put.

Again with the Honeysuckle

Birds in the background when I press *record* and I'm used to the sound of my own voice now.

Try as I might, I can't shake this feeling.

The peonies offer their usual suggestions, but I don't want that kind of love.

Instead, finally, I know what I know.

Someone wondered if it was suffering, but it wasn't.

When I stopped asking for stories, you told them better and more easily.

I'd rather be happy with you than without you. That's all.

Now I'm making a bow around the gift. When I look up, the sky is blue and the pines are green.

I Want Your Kisses

The metal tag on the sugar maple said *sugar maple*.

Likewise, I'm apprenticing myself to myself.

Saying that you try not to think of me is having it both ways.

When I trust enough to tell you, I get prettier.

Is this the fastest path to happiness, or is this happiness?

Beyond your shoulder, the hillside went dark for a minute.

What does it mean to be alive? We'll know when we're ready.

All Those Mysteries and All That

The forest where I was a little girl is on fire.
I had done my best hoping against hope there.
I had attended the church called *marriage*.

Used to be, a town could lay claim to a heart.
Once, the historical museum opened.
The future has never been anyone's business.

Some habitats go up in flames for good.
That's the truth of it. Not the worst thing.
My story held the first hundred times I told it.

It Was What It Was

And then it's a miracle. Or, the job of a miracle.
A good time to grow up. How exciting.

Now, the sound of it is your breath at my neck.
The picture book of it is a real page-turner.

Happiness isn't begged for, sweetheart;
that's my hand on your lap.

The kittens were having the time of their lives.
The glass reflected us as we were, only and exactly.

It's Tomorrow, Dear

Someone is setting off firecrackers in the street:
nothing to do with need.

I'm upstairs, choosing not to suffer much quietly:
again, no need.

What is common knowledge anyway?
The God I mentioned is the very same.

Men and I often hear failure where there is none.
Later, you hold me regardless.

I'm sitting in *enough already*, the spot reserved for me.
I can feel you waking on your side of town. No joke.

Today I like it here.
Don't tell, but the view is pretty damn good.

Acts of Experience

A hot May, and me working my lessons; I'd tell someone I'm
    done but what for.

Next door, a slow hammering: keeping up appearances three
    days in a row.

Someday I'll miss that shaggy pine if you want to know the
    truth of it.

Deeper into why, birds volleyed the simplest answer. A natural
    letdown.

Real love, too, is a series of dumb questions; will I come if
    called, for instance.

My heart took a day to decide; now I'm turning down the
    corner of the year.

June for Good

A Fine Romance, or Here's *Never* For You

Just about June, a light rain finishing, and now a few notes
from a guitar.

And somewhere you're walking the perimeter of what's to be
yours.

I've paced out love before, so I won't do that again, just so you
know.

Ahead of the dam, the river slugs along; after, the decision
takes over.

That's the reality of it. Why argue? Last year I knew what I
was asking.

And the shells you gathered and brought back were your lovely
answer.

These days I'm studying 1935: the phrasing of a song, the tilt
before a kiss.

What about you: sure you can't be pleased? You've looked
pleased plenty.

But who am I to say? Tomorrow, I'm going. More reality. Title:
June for Good.

Quite a Pink

The sunset proved impossible: a small, recurrent problem.

I want what I want and then I want more, usually.

Fear corresponds; there's no such thing as plain desire.

I re-read *Chapter Five: Shells* and consider my priorities.

A dark entrance deserves attention, I think we can agree.

The smell of fresh-cut grass is also a privilege, I remember.

You concede: you could be wrong. Joy comes naturally.

A Little Tawny Owl

I was choosing from among love's blue-greens.
Hard when I know a lake like each.

This is the very near future I'm attending.
Who's to say you're not aching also?

I was nearly gone once upon a time. Remember?
You waited with a view.

Turns out, every minute is the same length.
All the lessons in the world come to this.

Enough secrets.
The real heaven is steady; I found out for myself.

Little Noon

A year ago I did it differently; that's the gentlest way to put it.

The calendar gives no indication of how hard or easy.

I know I was alone a lot and not by choice.

This town is nothing but honeysuckle and catbirds. *Honestly.*

Correction: I chose, with a lake as my witness…

Life is mysterious until it's not; I've always been good at *so what.*

A tiny spider runs across my desk. Then another.

Tell me: what comes after a logical conclusion?

My Life in Heaven

This is a true account beginning now.

Here's a birch basket, tens of feathers, none of which will ever belong again.

This is like that, only more so.

Once I was a little girl who tried to write it.

Now I do twenty years' worth of looking every afternoon.

Like the insect that shed its *before* on the sand, and unstuck its wings, two pairs.

Time can't be wasted; some changes are forever.

The lake's three greens know, and its darker churning, and its eyelet edge.

Given the chance, I'd wear that to meet you.

The Deer Doesn't Go Looking for the Hunter

Today's hello is a minute of my afternoon recorded for your
    pleasure:
that sound is the wind thinking out loud to the lake;

I'm in the background, trying to decide.
Running away now just means someone's feelings got hurt
    back then.

Even the littlest swells know that.
In this way, childhood is the best dictionary ever invented.

In the shallows, the sand is scalloped: a series of gentle
    reminders:
pretty soon everything works out.

On Wednesday, I made Wednesday my home.
Now I'm practicing heartfelt action and inaction.

I want to believe in everlastingness.
One day includes so much; the sunset is anybody's guess.

A Quiet Tomorrow

I don't like it like this but I'll do it, I told the train whistle, the
    newly pink evening, anyone who would listen.

Unclaimed guilt sent me a pang.

Now I want to be the girl in the old-fashioned illustration who
    climbs a tree to meet the birds at eye level.

All my dreams are equally obvious: staircases and kissing.

Is there only one great chance? Have I changed you forever
    too? *Sweetheart—*

Little Muchness

I think one's art goes as far as one's love goes.

—Andrew Wyeth

Little Muchness

Some shouting and the tree came down branch by branch,
my *not so fast* a little late.

Now the wood burns and as usual I think my house is on fire.
Thus June ends.

What is with the world, I asked, and laid my cheek against the
     mantel.
I'm certainly not the first.

The sunset shrugs—*see ya*—and goes over the next-to-last
     mountain.
This is what not settling looks like.

I suppose a brave man might take this opportunity to get braver.
I'm done, so I'll wait in the kitchen.

I Would Welcome That

Everyone called it *a cleansing anger*. Like the wound that ran clear.

As of 2:07 p.m. I'm trying trust again, again.

Yes, I feel motion long after the fact. In bed beside you also.

It's an ache now not to introduce you to my feelings about the sunset.

Is it afternoon already, I asked the birthday.

Then remembered the best advice ever and resolved to soften.

Later, a slug on the sidewalk—striped—made me unaccountably happy.

What Remoteness

I pulled myself into myself, like a snail's personal mercy.
The fireworks finale was a different idea entirely;
I can't watch that, I said to no one listening.

Beneath the surface of the lake, a drowned waterfall.
What does *fairly painless* mean anyway?
Should I trust them or you, God or me?

In the regular forest, the sunlight was a just-OK idea.
In the river, a deer was testing the limits of *swerve now*.
Where I'm grown is lovely. I wrote that, just a moment ago.

Tending the Nectar

Little cracks in things.
Little anticipations.
The vase big as a balloon and shaped that way.

How will I ever get that home? was real.
The wind used all its verbs to answer.
I'm trying not to make the same mistakes.

Now a waiting feeling keeps me up.
Something greenish and delicate.
I'm confident but not that confident.

The smallest action is quite large.
The smallest appetite an appetite, still.
There's lots of brilliance.

Seeing myself in the floor-to-ceiling windows.
A picture of a bird discourages the real birds.
It's hard not to pose in this life.

Birch bark curls on the counter.
I can't learn fast enough.
The sunset, in my opinion, rushed the ending.

Knowing Full Well

One stone was black with a line of thought in it.
I began by tracing that.
And later, a small David I almost missed in the hollow of a tree.
Wind over the lake left sand for proof on my cheeks.
I liked it, so I kept it.
The deer too are calm in this season.
I myself had moved heaven and earth ages earlier.
Nothing much came of that.
And *who will notice me* was not the line as written but its meaning.
Every man was told to hang onto his own hope.
Eavesdropping, I thought to do the same.
Acres and acres sounds like tenderness to me now.
Come on, already.
Sometimes a little gesture takes the day.
Watching from here, I had often said, is no problem.

Two Things at Once

A late fawn and the lake as warm as I've ever known.

Everyone agrees well in advance: it'll be a hard winter.

But that's the future. My window is six panes for the present.

And haven't I said I prefer a grid? *Yes, but—*

Better yet, a body of water, something to set west.

Then, something to touch, furred or sueded, a color like that.

My sweeter self speaks up now; no more fussing at your collar.

Asked to hold an intention, I held radiant beauty.

No one inquired later whether or not it had come true.

Upon Reflection

Little August, August ago:
I could have saved myself a lot of heartache.
But that's not how I define the feminine.

A bad thing to say? I'm not sorry.
Recent illness brought me up close.
The woods were with me during the worst of it.

The fever *was* the house.
No one was coming was the truth.
I'm telling you so you know.

Each morning I choose a stone from the windowsill.
A calm instruction reminds me.
My ambition is to be wide open.

Notes

Some of these poems borrow language from *Science for Here and Now* by Herman and Nina Schneider, 2nd edition, 1965. Some borrow from *The Cambridge Introduction to Narrative* by H. Porter Abbott, 2002.

Alice Munro: the quotations come from "The Children Stay" and "Rich as Stink," respectively, both of which can be found in *The Love of a Good Woman* (Vintage, 1998).

Foo Fighters: "Learn to Fly."

Andrew Wyeth: *The Helga Pictures.*

Acknowledgments

Chronicle of Higher Education (online): "My Life in Heaven"

Colorado Review: "*At Glen Lake* vs. *The Birth of Anger*"

Connotation Press: An Online Artifact: "By the Way, *Hello*," "A Question and Its Answer," "Technological," "Two Things at Once"

Court Green: "In Answer to Your Burning Question"

Crazyhorse: "The Deer Doesn't Go Looking for the Hunter," "Little Muchness"

FIELD: "*Shark Shark Shark,* or Whatever It Is You Want Next," "A Painted Sun"

Jelly Bucket: "I Had My Castle Before You Had Your Fortress," "It's Not a Poem, It's a Novel," "In the Process of Making it Better," "A Covered Bridge," "Wouldn't It Be Dreamy"

The Journal: "All Those Mysteries and All That," "I Want Your Kisses," "It Was What It Was"

Kenyon Review: "Stupidity, Crabbiness, Moorings & Love"

Louisville Review: "Again with the Honeysuckle," "Some Kind of Lifetime"

Many Mountains Moving: "Happy Birthday, Everything!"

Mid-American Review: "The Key Is How," "Knowing Full Well," "This Is the Forest; Do You Like It?"

Passages North: "I'm Telling You the Story of Right Now," "It's Never Just a Minute with You"

POOL: "The Moon Through a Skylight," "Octoberish," "Speaking of Ferocity at Sunset," "You Can Thank Me Later," "You Got Your Wish; I Got Mine"

Truth Sauce: "Just Say When"

Wake: "Upon Reflection"